T0208294

WHEN A LOVED ONE DIES

Principles for Steering through Grief

SUSIE SANSOM-PIPER
WITH TAMARA S. POWELL

authorHOUSE®

AuthorHouse™
1663 Liberty Drive
Bloomington, IN 47403
www.authorhouse.com
Phone: 1 (800) 839-8640

Published by AuthorHouse 09/27/2019

Scripture quotations marked NIV are taken from the Holy Bible, New International Version®. NIV®. Copyright © 1973, 1978, 1984 by International Bible Society. Used by permission of Zondervan. All rights reserved. [Biblica]

Scripture quotations marked KJV are from the Holy Bible, King James Version (Authorized Version). First published in 1611. Quoted from the KJV Classic Reference Bible, Copyright © 1983 by The Zondervan Corporation.

Scripture taken from the New King James Version®. Copyright © 1982 by Thomas Nelson. Used by permission. All rights reserved

ISBN: 978-1-7283-2736-5 (sc)
ISBN: 978-1-7283-2735-8 (e)

Library of Congress Control Number: 2019914031

Print information available on the last page.

Part I

There are many descriptive words to articulate the feeling and lonliness experienced when facing death. They all seem to fall flat when emulating the true picture of the state of the heart and the emptiness of the mind and soul when a loved one dies.

For me, death stole in swiftly and unannounced. I faced death and broken-ness with the sudden death of my husband due to a massive heart attack while teaching school in another town. I had merely buried him and completed paying for his burial when in 1 month, ten days, my youngest daughter was killed in a tragic fiery car crash. I had no time to process. No time to mourn due to the horrific nature of her accident, I had to funeralize and bury her two days later. I was never even able to see her body. No closure. Moving through grief without thinking, walking unconsciously, I was left to raise my two small grandchildren. No husband, no help.

It was only by God's grace that I survived the ordeal and through the help and compassion of people who surrounded me. When death stole in, I had but one alternative… to keep moving forward through the fog that threatened to overtake me. To keep on going to raise my two grandbabies. To keep on going to support my parents. To keep on working, to support my family. To find a way to emerge from the hurt that would follow me all the days of my life. To find a way to exist with the pain that now became part of my daily existence. To keep my focus so that it did not overtake me with dark shadows of despair.

No one knows how one feels, when a loved one dies. My experience will be different from yours. My pain is different from yours. We can offer a few words, or just quietly be with you as you process. We can hold your hand, or hold your tissue when you cry. We can reminisce with you, or sit in your grief.

We can only *try* to be compassionate and loving towards one another and provide support where we can. We can pray for your comfort, healing, and peace, when a loved one dies.....

Susie E. Sansom-Piper

It has been my distinct honor and privilege to work on this project with my grandmother Susie Sansom-Piper. She has been my teacher, my caregiver, my hero, all of my life. She wrote the original booklet, on Pandora's Box leading to <u>When A Loved One Dies</u>, in 2002 to present to a group of Seniors. Since that time, it has been used in numerous churches and grief settings across the United States. Deciding to publish this as one of her many life works, led me to assist her in this effort and revise the original manuscript.

My experience with death began at the age of 4 with a premonition of my grandfather, Emzy James Sansom's death. It was followed soon after at age 5 with a vision of my mother, Eula Sansom Hebert's tragic demise in a fiery car crash. These visions of death *on* the date and times of the incidents caused me to know at an early age, that people leave, and we have no control or say in the matter. We can't stop it by being there. We can't stop it by alerting someone. We simply must deal with the aftermath. In my case, I envisioned the precise activities as If I were standing there on the side of the road, or at the bedside. Since that time, I have had many experiences where I predicted or saw the death of a loved one before it happened. I have lost many beloved family members and friends. As a

Christian, I am thankful that I know that we will see our loved ones again.

In November 2018, I lost my little brother, Emzy Jerome Hebert. It was the hardest moment that I can remember because it was up close and personal. I was the caregiver, the decision maker, the big sister. The hardest decision I've ever made- to let him go. Through his death, I had to summon a measure of strength, like never before.

I had no time to grieve as I had to take care of my brother's arrangements and affairs, and see after my grandmother who is now 98 years young.

It is through this experience, watching my incredible grandmother handle challenges my entire life, and the unplanned *opportunity* to contribute to this work that I lend my experience and contributions to this writing and to you all. I pray that some measure of what we have included will help you through the grieving process and enable you to pay it forward. God bless you all!

Tamara Powell

4

Life Goes On

In Him, we live and have our being.

Life goes On!

In Him, we must march to a given beat,

Life goes on!

From Infancy to early school age,

Life goes on!

Teenage to adulthood

Life goes on!

Families begin. Middle age comes.

Life Goes on!

Old Age...Retirement Years,

Life goes on!

Immobility, Illnesses, Death

Life goes on!

DEATH

Demise....end...dying....decease...passing ...
expiration....parting...

Termination....release....rest....extinction....mortality
in extremis

Cease

DEATH

Curtains….lights out….last roundup….finis….
Grim reaper….final show stopper…..
Sleeping…..eternal rest…
afterlife….fatality….oblivion….repose

DEATH

"When the soul shall emerge from its sheath" - Marcus Aurelius

"A black camel which kneels at the gate of all."
– Abd-El-Kader

"An eternal night" – Algeron Swinburne

"The undiscovered country" – Shakespeare

"The grand perhaps" – Robert Browning

"A pale horse" – The Bible

"The port where all may refuge find.
– William Alexander

DEATH

"The point of no return"….

"The never forgotten incidents of life"

The most misunderstood of human encounters"

.…Susie Sansom-Piper

PANDORAS BOX

Things we may encounter or feel when a loved one dies.

Heartache   Pain

Grief   Illness

Depression   Worry

Loneliness   Financial Woes

Sorrow   Emotions   Greed

Self-Pity

Hatred

Anger

Emptiness

Jealousy

Anxiety

Isolation

Pity

Insecure

Relief

Guilt

Panic

Disbelief

Betrayed

Bewilderment

Peace

Shock

Fatigue

<u>Other Emotions/Words</u>

Take a Moment to Jot Down a Few Words to Describe your feelings when your loved one died. Do the words on the preceding page resonate with you? Were you expecting death or was it sudden and tragic?

Thought

"Death is not a period, but a comma in the story of life." – A, Tarver

KEEP ON KEEPING ON

There comes a time in everyone's life when everything you do seems to bring a measure of heartaches, discontent, and moments of sadness. Life just seems to turn upside down, and it often seems as if there is no place to go and nowhere to turn. But there is always hope. There is always the light at the end of the tunnel, and it is up to us to find the hope that will keep us keeping on.

That hope that "keeps us keeping on" is found in the Divine Word. It is up to us trust in this Word to help see us through the "upside downs" of our life.

One way to manifest and increase our hope or faith is to meditate on Jesus. "For God so loved the world that He gave his only begotten Son, that whosever believeth in Him shall not perish, but have everlasting life." John 3:16 KJV

Just as Jesus had compassion on the two blind men who sat by the way side as he was enroute to the City of Jerusalem, and healed them of their blindness, we as Christians, should also show our compassion and concern for others.

When we are concerned, our attention or interest, care is energized, and we become aware of the effect of the particular matter on individuals' welfare and happiness.

Concern implies an anxious sense of interest in, or responsibility for something. When we have compassion, we manifest a deep sympathy and sorrow for another's suffering or misfortune, and we are moved with a feeling of tenderness to help alleviate their suffering.

Galatians 6:2 says, "Bear ye one another's burdens". You can share someone's burdens with a word of kindness, a listening ear, or a word of advice. You can lessen the burden of the needy through various contributions. You can brighten the day of someone in need by sending a card, writing a letter, a small gift, or a short visit.

Make an effort to share your experiences with others so that they know they are not alone. Offer your heart and give of yourself, your love, your time. This not only will help you to heal, but also heal others and sow seeds of joy and gratitude in their heart. The positive seeds which you sow into the lives of others will bring joy and abundant blessings into your own. In spite of a world of turbulence, heartache, and unrest, one thing is certain, we can be assured that we can safely rely on God for his divine guidance and wisdom in leading us into the unforeseen future.

Our mental outlook must be concentrated on our service to God. We should also remember that as Christians, our loved ones, who are saved, merely sleep until the coming of Christ and we shall see them again. Although this does not lessen the grief and pain in our humanness, we must hold to God's word and must not copy the behavior and customs of the world.

Within each of us, there is a God-given ability to do certain things well. Through your heartache, experiences, living, you may share life with others. It is our Christian duty to perform and give our best with spirits of cheerfulness, humility, and eagerness. We are told to be genuine in our love for one another, hate that which is evil, and stand for that which is good. Where there is hope, rejoice. Where there is pain and tribulation, be patient and prayerful always. When others are happy, be happy with them. When they are sad, share in their sorrow.

Make an effort to meditate on God's word. Pull off and throw away those clothes of anger, despair, guilt, melancholy, depression, worry, grief, frustration, greed, panic, and all of the other invisible emotions attached to your loss of a loved one.

I know that it is not easy. Some of those feelings will never go away; however, God will unburden our hearts when we look to him, bind his word in our hearts, and are willing to wear new clothes.

How do we begin? We can take steps towards the new day. Putting one foot in front of the other every day.

Sometimes after a loss, the world appears dull.

How can the sun still shine?

How are people laughing and playing?

Don't they know the hurt I am feeling? Don't they know our mother, father, brother, sister, child, or significant other is no longer with us? Our lives have changed forever without the presence of our loved one lost. How can I even get up tomorrow? Everything feels desensitized, so, now what?

LIFT

Lift your eyes to our Father in Heaven. He will help us to overcome, if we follow his word. Sometimes when we are down, we have a tendency to bow our heads and hunch our shoulders. This posture serves to pull us lower and lower. With downcast eyes, we can get lost in our thoughts and sadness. We don't see those in front of us who would attempt to lift our spirits and ignore offers of help.

Pray and meditate on his word that you may find contentment, satisfaction, peace, and delight. He will keep us in his care, in spite of the hard times we face. We can find happiness again in his presence.

I cannot say that you or I will go back to where we were before the loss of our loved one, but we can find a different state of happiness. A different state of content. A different way of existing as we LIFT our eyes and hearts to the Lord.

> *Psalms 121-"I will lift up my eyes to the hills,*
> *From which cometh my help?*
> *My help comes from the Lord*
> *Who made heaven and earth*
> *He will not allow your foot to be moved;*
> *He who keeps you will not slumber.*

Behold, He who keeps Israel
Shall neither slumber nor sleep.
The Lord is your keeper;
The Lord is your shade at your right hand.
The sun shall not strike you by day,
Nor the moon by night.
The Lord shall preserve you from evil
He shall preserve your soul.
The Lord shall preserve your going out and
your coming in.
From this time forth, and even forevermore."
(NIV)

How can I lift my eyes when I am suffering? Suffering means to undergo or feel pain or stress, to undergo a penalty, or to undergo or experience agony and torment. Suffering can be physical or mental. Physical anguish may be felt at the loss of a love. One may experience illness, pain, or injuries while grieving. Mental sufferings can cause one to feel that they are under judgement, persecuted, criticized, or feeling mental agony. They question has often been asked- "Why do Christians suffer?"

According to man, this should not be because the Christians are true believers and followers of Christ. Through our sufferings, we must be aware of the protection of Christ. We must know and believe that he intercedes on our behalf and no trials have fallen on us that he himself did not endure.

Psalms 31:23-24 states: O love the Lord, all ye his saints, for the Lord preserveth the faithful, and plentifully rewardeth the proud doer. Be of good courage and he shall strengthen your heart, all ye that hope in the Lord. (KJV)

Psalms 34:18 The Lord is near to the brokenhearted and saves the crushed in spirit. (NIV)

Therefore, Lift your face to the sun and the heavens. Open your heart to the Lord. Offer your emotions and feelings to him. Ask for help. Share your heart and sorrows with others. Take steps everyday to lift your spirits.

CAST

Cast when worried. Cast when troubled. Cast when depressed.

God wants to take care of us, but in order to let Him, we must stop taking the care. We must put down the baggage, the heavy load and let him carry it for us.

How does casting help me find happiness, when I have lost my loved one? I don't think I will ever smile or be happy again.

Happiness is a state of contentedness, delight, enjoyment, and satisfaction. Delight is happiness that expresses a degree of joy and rapture. *Enjoyment* is experiencing happiness with pleasure and satisfaction. All of these forms of happiness can belong to those who are in Christ Jesus.

> *I Peter 5:6-7, "Therefore humble yourselves under the mighty hand of God, that He may exalt you in due time, casting all your care on Him, for He cares for you." (NKJV)*

Casting our cares on the Lord helps to bring us peace.

Focus your minds on the good things of life. The positive memories and presence of your loved one.

Spiritual peace comes when we acquaint ourselves with the Lord. The fruit of the spirit is love, joy, and peace. Put your trust in God, and He will grant to you those things that are needed to move forward in life.

An Exercise in Casting Your Cares:

Take a moment to write down your worries.

Write your prayer and let your requests be known to God.

What fears are you harboring regarding the loss of your loved one?

What good thoughts can you focus on in the present moment?

THINK

What does worrying accomplish? Have you or I ever been able to accomplish anything by worrying about it? How does worry affect you?

When we are worried, fretful and in despair or desperation, our bodies do not function properly. These fight or flight responses of the mind or our mental heart, can affect our overall health, and contribute largely to the health of our physical bodies. Negative thoughts and stress creates physical stress on the body. *Worry is a kind of disease that can cause other diseases such as high blood pressure and heart failure.* It is imperative that one keeps our mental heart free of destructive and damaging thoughts. It is imperative to quiet our minds and rest in the meditation of God's word to strengthen and keep us through our sorrow.

Worry is a destructive force. Worry will soon produce fear. It is a burden, a load that is carried unconsciously, and even sometimes inflicted on others.

Worry can also be self-punishment. Worry will destroy the mind, the thoughts, and eventually cause mental suicide. Worry will rob you of your faith, take away any inner peace, and make you have a lack of trust in God.

Worry will not change what has happened or what is to be, we cannot stop or change the course.

This reminds me of a favorite saying of my mother's "Whatever will be, will be."

> *Can any one of you, by worrying, add a single hour to your life? (Matthew 6:27) (NIV)*
>
> *Therefore, do not worry about tomorrow, for tomorrow will worry about itself. Each day has enough trouble of its own. (Matthew 6:34)NIV*

We are what we think! Our actions comply with our thoughts. Our countenance reflects our thoughts just as the mirror reflects the way we look.

PRAY

Prayer is a communication between man and God. It is a means of opening the heart and soul to the Almighty, and to one who understands our needs and our wants. It is an invitation to live with God and worship in him. It is an expression of submission to His will, and a means of giving praise.

The bible tells us to pray without ceasing. Our prayers should be given with faith and belief. It is okay to pray without knowing exactly what to say. God knows what we need before we express it and he will answer us in due time.

Prayer and meditation on God's word allows us to not only lift our eyes to him, cast our worries and cares; but, also gives opportunity for God to communicate with us and align our thinking with his word. It is the most powerful resource that we possess. Not only is it direct communication with God, but it is a means by which we can ask God to grant us our desires. But, at the same time, we must recognize that prayer must be offered in faith, asking that His Will be done and not our will.

Sometimes you may find it difficult just to get through the day. You may not feel that you have strength to pray. Sometimes one's mind is plunged into an abyss of darkness and the soul is deprived of the light of the world. With God, there is power unlimited… a power that can never be shut off or destroyed, if we give ourselves over to him.

Just stop and pray. Asking God for help, for wisdom, and for strength, will help to renew your mind and spirit in the midst of tragedy.

He gives strength to the weary and increases
the power of the weak. (Isaiah 40:29 NIV)

There will be plenty of times that you don't know what to do or how to respond to your problems. Prayer in the midst of trouble helps us see God again. It gets our eyes off of our problems and focuses us afresh on God who is all powerful, merciful, and just.

Use your prayer power in all of your daily undertakings.

James 1:5 – *"If any of you lacks wisdom,*
he should ask God." (KJV)

POSITIVE ATTITUDE

Keep a positive attitude...no hesitating...no doubting... take your concerns to the Lord. Many people operate with zero power because they are always mixing the positive with the negative.

The Christian attitude is to think thankful thoughts each and every day. Even in the midst of trouble, be thankful for being able to breathe freely. Be thankful for the days of adversity, trials, and tribulations, for it is sometimes that we experience these hardships in order to bring out the good things in us.

Saturate your minds with constant gratitude and look for reasons to be thankful. Think thankful and positive thoughts.

Do not be anxious about anything, but in every situation, by prayer and petition, with thanksgiving, present your requests to God. And the peace of God which surpasses all understanding will guard your hearts and minds through Christ Jesus. (Phillipians 4:6-7) NIV

For I know the plans I have for you, declares the Lord, plans for welfare and not for evil, to give you a future and hope. (Jeremiah 29:11) (NIV)

TRUST

If we trust God, we can meet the miseries and disappointments of life. Nothing is impossible with God. With trust, comes Faith. Faith is confidence in God. It is believing his word, that he will do what he said.

Faith is Trusting. It brings inner peace because it is obtained through our trusting. Faith is security – a security that can only be obtained through acceptance of whatever God has in store for us. Faith is eternal.

Psalms 37: 3 – "Trust in the Lord, and do good; dwell in the land, and feed on His faithfulness." (NKJV)

Proverbs 3: 5— "Trust in the Lord with all your heart, And lean not on your own understanding. In all your ways acknowledge Him, And He shall direct your path." (NKJV)

BE CAREFUL WHOM YOU TRUST:

"Do not trust in a friend; Do not put your confidence in a companion; Guard the doors of your mouth. From her who lies in your bosom." (Micah 7: 5)

Be careful, and do not allow ANXIETY to enter into your life. Trust in the Lord in all things and just "keep on keeping on."

"Anxiety in the heart of a man causes depression, But a good word makes it glad." Proverbs 12:25 (NKJV)

Particularly when grieving the loss of a loved one, emotions can run high between family and friends. Well intended words, often misplaced, in the midst of grief can cause strife and hurt feelings. It is imperative to protect your words and heart during this difficult time. This is a time that is crucial for protecting your family unit. It is here that many family members stop speaking and communicating, some, unfortunately for decades. Misunderstandings and cross words due to grief and stress.

Eliminate the anxiety. It only tends to make you more uneasy, filled with dread, and will sometimes produce evil thoughts or works. In other words, one may over react to certain situations.

PATIENCE AND PERSEVERANCE

James 1: 2-4... *"Count it all joy when you fall into various trials, knowing that the testing of your faith produces patience. But let patience have its perfect work, that you may be perfect and complete, lacking nothing. "* **(NKJV)**

Be patient with yourself and others. As days pass, your sense of loss may dull or you may have fleeting moments of happiness; but, the loss will still remain. Grief and the process of grieving is different for everyone. Everyone experiences the emotions differently.

Endurance or Patience is important. One must have the strength to endure and the patience to understand whatever trials and tribulations that may confront us. God is a most understanding God, and He never overburdens us with more than we are able to endure. Even though we may feel at times that we are at the end of the road.

In due time, things will get better for you, if you have patience and endurance. Nothing comes to fruition overnight.

ANGER AND BITTERNESS

Do not allow anger to enter into your hearts when certain situations confront you. Anger destroys you, and produces fear as well as a certain amount of bitterness. Ask yourself, am I bitter? Whatever you are going through; use the power of positive thinking to get you through.

Through the power of thought, inventions have been perfected, nuclear weapons have been developed, man has been to the moon. Through the power of thought, we can develop ourselves into people of power or position.

If anger and bitterness are allowed to take root in our minds or hearts, the same greatness and power can turn to hatred, jealousy, bitterness and despair. Deal with anger before it causes you to do or say something you will regret. Pray for peace of mind.

Refrain from anger and turn from wrath;
do not fret- it leads only to evil.
Psalms 37:8 NIV

Better a patient person than a warrior, one with sel-
control than one who takes a city. (Proverbs16:32 NIV)

CHOICES

We have a choice. We have free will. We can stop living at the loss of our loved one because the grief is too much to bear. We feel as though we cannot go on. We can choose to live on and cherish the memory and blessings of having our loved one in our lives for a brief time.

Choose Life. Choose your favorite scripture, one that gives you comfort. Memorizing and praying through these scriptures will be helpful in anchoring or bringing stability to your life.

What are some of the scriptures that give you peace or reassurance? Jot them down and meditate on or memorize a few every day. In my time of loss, I read the 23rd Psalms every night before bed.

For you, it might be reading or reciting before work. It might be posted on your bathroom mirror. You may write it in lipstick on the mirror. You might choose a bulletin board on your refrigerator or a sticky note on your car dash.

Wherever you can stop for a moment to recite a comforting word from God will strengthen your heart and mind for that moment, that hour, and that day.

When you feel like crying, Cry. When you feel like grieving, Grieve. There is no timetable. There is no clock. There is no date that we can say the pain will dissipate. We just keep moving forward day by day. Make the choice.

CONFIDENCE

In times of trouble, we must resist the question marks of *Why*, and concentrate on *Who*. Once we understand whom it is that stands besides us in trouble, our confidence will be strong. When we trust in Him, He will teach us how to triumph in our pain and sorrows.

Have you not known? Have you not heard? The everlasting God, the Lord, The Creator of the ends of the earth, Neither faints nor is weary. His understanding is unsearchable. He gives power to the weak, And to *those* who have no might He increases strength, Even the youths shall faint and be weary, And the young men shall utterly fall, But those who wait on the lord shall renew *their* strength; they shall mount up with wings like eagles, They shall run and not be weary, They shall walk and not faint. Isaiah 40:28-31 (NKJV)

BLOOM WHERE YOU ARE PLANTED

Don't look back on the past for comfort and security. Nothing you say or do can change the past. God uses tragedy in our lives to awaken us to many things. He will be there with His Word for you, His Promises, and His Provisions.

We must remember that no one is exempt. No area of life is out of bounds.

Sooner or later, we are all faced with the loss of loved ones. But if we trust God, He will use our troubles to produce character, competency, and endurance to overcome.

JOY COMES IN THE MORNING

Today, it may seem that you will never feel again.

Today, it may seem that you will never experience life again.

It's true. Your life, my life has changed forever. No amount of sympathy, no truckload of cards, no mountain of food will ease the ache of losing a loved one. BUT, Joy does come in the morning.

One day, you will wake up and the pain is not as severe.

One day, you will make it through the day or hour without bursting into tears, or choking back your emotions. One day, you will have a memory of your loved one that makes you smile instead of sink into depression. One morning it will come.

We have the following assurances from the Holy Bible:

For His anger is but for a moment, His favor is for life;
Weeping may endure for a night, But joy
comes in the morning. Psalms 30: 5 (KJV)

So do not fear, for I am with you; do not be dismayed,
for I am your God. I will strengthen you and help you;
I will uphold you with my righteous
right hand. Isaiah 41:10 (NIV)

He heals the brokenhearted and binds up
their wounds (Psalms 147:3) (NIV)

And finally, the assurance that those of us left behind, will see our loved ones who are asleep in Christ once again.

Brothers and sisters, we do not want you to be
uninformed about those who sleep in death, so that
you do not grieve like the rest of mankind, who have no
hope. For we believe that Jesus died and rose again, and
so we believe that God will bring with Jesus those who
have fallen asleep in him. According to the Lord's word,
we tell you that we who are still alive, who are left until
the coming of the Lord, will certainly not precede those
who have fallen asleep. For the Lord himself will come
down from heaven with a loud command, with the voice
of the archangel, and with the trumpet call, and the dead
in Christ will rise first. After that, we who are still alive
and are left, will be caught up together with them in the
clouds to meet the Lord in the air. And so we will always
be with the Lord forever. Therefore encourage one
another with these words. (1 Thessalonians 4:13-18 NIV)

FOR THOSE LEFT BEHIND

"Blessed are they that mourn: for they shall
be comforted." – Matthew 5:4…. (KJV)

The death of a loved one is always painful for the survivors. There are many conflicting emotions that must be dealt with. Be willing to accept sympathetic help from friends and relatives, for they can help ease the pain.

When accepting help from others, Kathryn Wilson says to remember:

- **TRUE COMFORT IS NOT PITY.**
- **LET THE BEREAVED KNOW THAT THEY ARE NOT ALONE.** Loneliness is the greatest fear of all.
- **LET THE BEREAVED "TALK IT OUT."** Be a good listener.
- **LET THE BEREAVED WEEP** with the assurance that grief is normal and healthy.
- **DON'T PRETEND THAT NOTHING HAS CHANGED. IT HAS!** Sometimes the bereaved is reluctant to admit it.

When Helping the Grieving

IF YOU SEE A NEED, take care of it.

Examples.... *Transportation, laundry, errands, baby-sitting, messages, phone calls, etc. may be needed.*

SPREAD YOUR OFFERS OF HELP and encouragement in days that are yet to come.

People often disappear after the service is over. It is the long days following that those who have lost a loved one really need help. Reach out, even if it is just to say I am thinking of you.

Don't ask how they are feeling. What are they supposed to say?

"I am hurting". I can't stop crying. I can't stop thinking. I hate my life right now. No one understands!

Don't tell them to get over it or pack things up, give them away, change their answering machine! They may not be ready. Everyone moves forward in their own time.

There is no easy way to mourn our loved ones. Only the passage of time can heal the pain of loss. For those who are there to help, be sure to make your presence felt in tactful, practical ways.

We must always remember that death is a fact of life. We cannot ignore, deny or avoid the thought, of death. It is the end of earthly existence as we know it. It can be viewed as a way to union with God and an end to suffering.

Paul says: "For me to live is Christ, and to die is gain." - Philippians 1:21 (KJV)

Translated: "Life to me, of course, is Christ. He is the reason to live; but then death would bring me something more for I will be with him in eternity.

Express your grief, but underline it with faith and hope for the dawning of a new life.

Part II

Loss....

The act of losing... the harm or privation resulting from loss or separation...a person or thing or an amount that is lost.....destruction.....puzzled....state of distress.

LOST....

Unable to find the way... no longer visible... helpless...adrift...astray
Ruined... destroyed... desperate... no longer possessed...

LIVE....

To be alive....to maintain oneself....to exhibit vigor, gusto, or enthusiasm....to attain eternal life....to remain in human memory or record....

LOVE....

An affection based on admiration or benevolence....
unselfish concern that freely accepts another in
loyalty and seeks his good;
Brotherly concerns for others...to like or desire
actively...

LOVING KINDNESS

Tender and benevolent affection...
Considerate consciousness
inclination towards affection....
Compassion and empathy...

PATHWAYS THROUGH GRIEF

People say: "Time heals." Yet time by itself, doesn't heal...it is what we do with time that can heal.

Rev. Arnaldo Pangrazzi

<<<<<<<<<<>>>>>>>>>>

We are all experts when it comes to grief. At some point in our lives, someone we love dies, and we wonder how we will go on...how we will get up and go to work and how we will pay bills..... how we'll ever laugh or enjoy life again when this person who means so much to us is gone. Traveling through grief is not easy. We have to learn to accept our feelings.... Sadness, anger, guilt, loneliness, confusion, fear... denial...sleeplessness or sleeping too much... loss of interest in everything...smoking intensely or using alcohol or drugs.... Etc.

NO ONE GRIEVES ALIKE

Everyone grieves differently because every death may be different. This is a time some may succumb to many of the harmful behaviors listed.

No one grieves the Wrong Way. There is no perfect plan or path for grief. But, it is important to refrain from self-destructive behavior and be kind and patient with yourself.

Seven Principles for Steering Through Grief

1. _Accept our grief_ and face our emotions. We will then realize that it is possible to keep the memory of our loved ones alive without being mired in despair.

2. _Pray often_. Prayer can help lead those in grief to a place of both remembering the good things about a loved one, and at the same time, gradually letting go.

3. _Remember_ that "Life goes on for the living." We must re-create our lives. We never really say goodbye. But we change our relationship from the physical side of life to a spiritual connection.

4. _Relieve the pain_ of grieving by remembering the fun times you had together.

5. _Acknowledge that "it's alright_ to grieve." Cry when you so desire

6. _Write down memories_ of your loved ones that you cherish most. Think of the attributes you most admired in your loved one.

7. _Use your sorrows_ to help other grieving people.

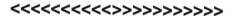

Alan Paon said: "Jesus suffered...not to save us from suffering, but to teach us how to bear suffering."

He reveals our ultimate dependence on him despite our circumstances.

Those who are suffering can comfort others in deep and unique ways. 2 Corinthians 1:3-5

SCRIPTURES

Psalm 27:1   Psalm 55:22   Psalm 121
Isaiah 49:13   John 14:27 II   Corinthians 1:3-4
Psalms 147:3   I Peter 5:10   Revelations 21:4
                Revelations 7:17

No matter what, God will give you peace in the midst of your struggles. Trust Him!

RE-INVENT YOURSELF

Somewhere in your life, or your period of grief, you will have to come to the realization that you have to move on, move past the state you are in, and renew your outlook on life in general.

It's true, your faith is often shaken; but, through it all, some way, some how, you have to turn the "inward suffering" into an "overcoming and joyful period of life. Look for the good things in your life, although they may be based on your past life

Enjoy the gifts that God has given you.

Use your talents to help others. It may be helping elderly and homeless people. You may enjoy sewing, cooking, and mentoring little children.

Visit the nursing homes. Many of these individuals often are all alone. Take a small gift to them, and then get your joy from watching the smiles on their faces.

STOP and realize, that you need to "love yourself", and that you need to give yourself that special personal attention... could be wholesome

WHEN A LOVED ONE DIES

thoughts...new friends, new surroundings, whatever it takes, to make a new "you".

Whatever it takes to help you face your new life without the one you love.

Remember... no two individuals are alike.

No one will grieve alike, but through your unshakeable faith, you can say to yourself: "I can."

And through your belief in God, you will find yourself able to say: "I will". The result will be that you find yourself again and discover a unique new you.

SUGGESTIONS FOR EASING THE PAIN OF A LOSS

The death of a loved one is painful for the survivors. Sympathetic relatives and friends can ease the pain of loss.

1. Remember true comfort is not pity.

2. Your role is to assure the bereaved that they are not alone, the greatest fear of all of us.

3. Be a good listener. Let them "talk it out." Listen to your friends; let them tell you how they feel.

4. Let him weep; assure him that grief is normal and healthy.

5. Be there. Go to the home for a visit, even if you only stop by for a few minutes and go to the service. It provides immeasurable support and comfort.

6. Be honest. If you don't know what to say, don't be afraid to say so.

7. If you see a need, take care of it. Transportation, laundry, errands, baby-sitting, messages, phone calls, etc.

8. Spread your offers of help and encouragement over days to come.

9. Send a card, note or letter with a handwritten note expressing your sorrow and sharing your fond memories of the person who died.

10. Don't judge. Everybody grieves in his or her own way. Don't tell them not to cry. Don't assume It's for the best. Don't say, "I know how you feel." no matter what your experience has been. Don't rush them through the grieving process, it is in their own time.

11. Be awkward. If you don't know what to say, just be. Just sit. Don't feel the need to fill awkward silence.

LOSS

The word L-O-S-S carries with it many kinds of losses... losing one's friend...losing property or money....losing one's mind.... Losing a loved one through natural or unnatural death,

But
it all amounts to
something that is hard for you to recover from,
something that has caused you deep
distress and unhappiness,
OR
something that you will never recover.
This L-O-S-S produces grief and distress.

My experience in life has encountered this l-o-s-s by death, through various causes:

1. Loss of first husband by sudden or unexpected death
2. Loss of daughter two years later via automobile accident
3. Loss of father by natural causes.

4. Loss of mother by natural causes.

5. Loss of second husband by natural causes.

6. Loss of the grandson I raised.

Each death brought about traumatic changes in my life, and many unexpected experiences which I had to overcome. But the good news is that through the help of the Master, you can find your way!

LIFE DOES NOT END FOR YOU.

You've got to maintain yourself. You have a job to do. You've got to renew your enthusiasm. I read each morning and each night the 23rd Psalms and the 121st Psalms.

It was through the fourth L-o-s-s- that I renewed the love in my life, for God has always been the love of my life. There came into my life much unselfish concern for my well- being, and through this I have learned to share my love with others, for life goes on.

When a Loved One Dies, we extend our most sincere sympathy for your loss. We pray that you find peace. We pray that you find peace as you walk through this journey. May the Lord bless and keep you, grant you serenity, healing, and strength.

A Word

At some point in my life, I have endured tremendous sufferings, not bodily sufferings, but mental sufferings. I have experienced all of the troubles that are in Pandora's Box, but through my belief in God and His Word, I have overcome. I count it all joy for the longevity God has given me, and I count it all joy that He has given me the strength to endure and to overcome the fallacies of life. Adopt the motto: "I will be tough on the outside, yet tender on the inside," and it will not be difficult to endure.

You too, can overcome. Walk daily with the Master.

Walk with character, integrity, and lift your head high in the face of difficulties. But as for me, "I trust in you, O Lord; I say, "You are my God."

The Author
Susie Sansom Piper

Printed in the United States
By Bookmasters

Printed in the United States
By Bookmasters